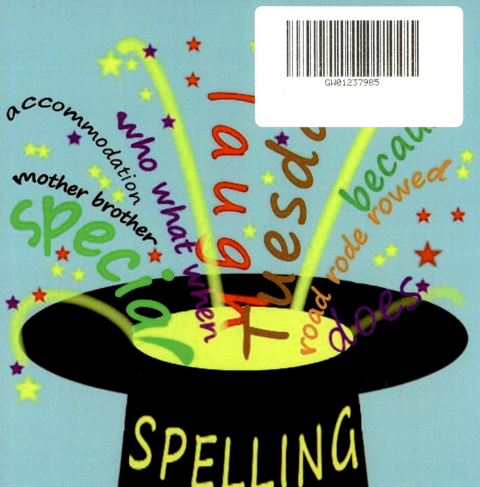

accommodation
mother brother
special
who what when
laugh
Tuesday
because
road rode rowed
does

SPELLING TRICKS for CHILDREN

by Sally Raymond

Sally Raymond works with children, teachers, parents and adult students, helping them discover strategies which support the development of their confidence, memory, personal engagement and learning.

Qualified as a dyslexia specialist, Sally recognises the importance of success over failure. She champions the use of varied teaching and learning strategies to suit individual needs, promoting opportunities for engagement, achievement and diversity.

"Not everyone will need the spelling tricks contained in this book, but for those that do, I hope you find them effective, fun and easy to use."

Sally Raymond DipSpLD(Hornsby), QTLS, PGDip(SEN)

Spelling Tricks for Children

© 2016 Sally Raymond

Published by Dragonfly Teaching.

sally@dragonflyteaching.org

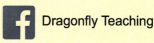

Dragonfly Teaching

Spelling Tricks for Children

First published in Great Britain by Dragonfly Teaching 2016
www.dragonflyteaching.org   sally@dragonflyteaching.org

© 2016 Sally Raymond

ISBN 978-0-9954769-0-5

Cover and content illustrations by S. Collard
Additional illustrations by L. Collard

Printed in the United Kingdom

This book is dedicated to Tia, Tazmin, Robert and Rosie... and to everyone who enjoys using these spelling tricks.

A number of English words have tricky spellings...

The word might be spelled differently from the sound of its letters:

'Was', 'said', 'does', 'many' and 'what' do not sound how they look.

You might have a choice between spelling patterns which make the same sound:

The words 'bird', 'heard', 'herd', 'stirred', 'word' and 'purred' all contain the same sound.

Some words sound the same, but have different meanings:

'Wait' / 'weight', 'blue' / 'blew', 'by' / 'buy' are all homophones.

There may be silent letters in a spelling which can trip you up:

'Thumb', 'head', 'scissors', 'island' and 'guide' contain silent letters.

Additional information for parents and teachers can be found in *Spelling Rules, Riddles and Remedies* by Sally Raymond (Routledge publishers).

Helpful Advice

Pick a spelling trick which suits your needs, studying up to five patterns during one week.

Let your brain SEE and STUDY the prompt. How might it help you avoid making spelling errors?

Move everything out of sight before making your own copy of the spelling prompt in the frame provided, or into a book of your own.

You can look back to the prompt if you want, but TAKE YOUR TIME to study it first to reduce the number of times you need to look at it again.

Within the next 12 hours, test yourself on the prompt and its spelling. This second visit helps to transfer information from short-term memory into long-term memory. If you have forgotten the spelling prompt or the spelling, look back to the original trick (adapt it if you want to), and repeat the copying process above.

Over the following seven days, test yourself on your spellings and their prompts. Play DICEY SPELLINGS, applying one action to each word every time you play.

The brain likes pictures. Visual images are often recalled more easily than letters.

The trick is to use colour, amusement, meaning, familiarity and purpose to nudge the brain away from making common spelling mistakes.

A GOOD SPELLING TRICK
must always relate to the
MEANING OF THE WORD

When writing, the brain triggers a word's meaning (e.g.WHAT?) and fires the prompt's pathway lodged in the memory through the use of varied processing activities (see *'underlying principles for teachers'*).

'WHAT an amazing <u>hat</u>!'

The aim is to learn a tricky spelling by <u>remembering the memory prompt</u> which steers the mind away from making a mistake.

DICEY SPELLINGS

This game strengthens memory pathways. First, explore the role of each letter in a word. Where, and why, might a spelling mistake be made? Use a spelling trick to avoid errors. Then put everything out of sight. Throw a dice. Perform one of the following activities:

1   Spell word aloud, with your eyes shut
2   Write word, with your eyes shut
3   Write word using your opposite hand
4   Write word using bubble writing
5   Draw / write the spelling prompt
     ... and then explain it in a silly voice
6   Sing a sentence containing the word

adapted from *Spelling Rules, Riddles and Remedies* (Routledge)

Explore a spelling trick.
What is it doing?
Why is it doing it?
When you are ready, move
everything out of sight.
Draw your own copy of the
spelling trick from memory.
Now speak a sentence.
Write down the target
word(s) when you say them.
The aim is to link a spelling
PROMPT to words whose
tricky spellings might try
to trip us up.
Play Dicey Spellings to
practise different words.

CONTENTS

Draw a copy of spelling prompts from memory. Then cover your work before writing down the target word(s). Play Dicey Spellings to secure the new prompt pathways.

Spelling Tricks for Children by Sally Raymond

Can you w**alk**
and **talk** about
lovable **k**ittens?

I can s**ee**
you are
asl**ee**p

Draw a copy of spelling prompts from memory. Then cover your work before writing down the target word(s). Play Dicey Spellings to secure the new prompt pathways.

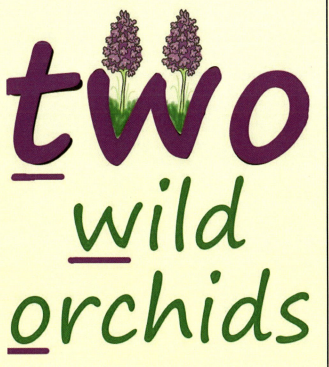

_t_wo
_w_ild
_o_rchids

ēyē

Draw a copy of spelling prompts from memory. Then cover your work before writing down the target word(s). Play Dicey Spellings to secure the new prompt pathways.

It <u>was</u> a surprise to...

see...

hear...

find...

smell...

Invent your own sentences. Draw a picture for each one.

I want to be an ant.

Draw a copy of spelling prompts from memory. Then cover your work before writing down the target word(s). Play Dicey Spellings to secure the new prompt pathways.

I **like** to kiss e!

are

<u>a</u>ardvarks <u>r</u>eally ext<u>r</u>aterrestrials?

Spelling Tricks for Children by Sally Raymond

15

Draw a copy of spelling prompts from memory. Then cover your work before writing down the target word(s). Play Dicey Spellings to secure the new prompt pathways.

p e o p l e

The pe-op-le
are the people
who speak with
spelling voices.

Big elephants
can always
understand
small elephants
because
they speak the
same language.

Spelling Tricks for Children by Sally Raymond

17

Draw a copy of spelling prompts from memory. Then cover your work before writing down the target word(s). Play Dicey Spellings to secure the new prompt pathways.

their cat

Their cat
likes to sit
on their
fence post
outside their
house.

Her Olephant
was here.

... here, there
and everywhere!

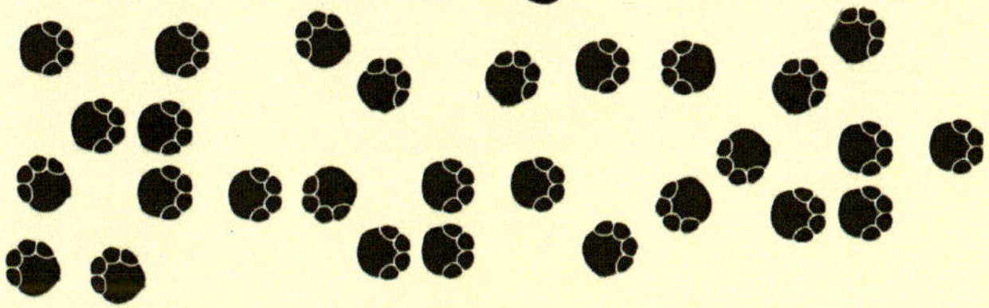

Draw a copy of spelling prompts from memory. Then cover your work before writing down the target word(s). Play Dicey Spellings to secure the new prompt pathways.

Use the prompt you like best.

Are you
SURE
small unicorns
really exist?

Are you
SURE U R Eating
sugar, not salt?

Use white sugar and salt to add the experience of taste to this memory prompt.

Spelling Tricks for Children by Sally Raymond

21

Draw a copy of spelling prompts from memory. Then cover your work before writing down the target word(s). Play Dicey Spellings to secure the new prompt pathways.

What's that **noise?**
It's only a tortoise blowing its nose.

noise

I'm an **important ant !**

Draw a copy of spelling prompts from memory. Then cover your work before writing down the target word(s). Play Dicey Spellings to secure the new prompt pathways.

What an amazing hat!

Who...
will hear owl?

Draw a copy of spelling prompts from memory. Then cover your work before writing down the target word(s). Play Dicey Spellings to secure the new prompt pathways.

DOES Ollie eat snails?

Yes, he does. YUK!

Hey! They have eaten Yumyum!

Spelling Tricks for Children by Sally Raymond

27

Draw a copy of spelling prompts from memory. Then cover your work before writing down the target word(s). Play Dicey Spellings to secure the new prompt pathways.

Seven out <u>of ten</u>...
that's <u>often</u>.

Sally-<u>A</u>nn <u>is</u> <u>dead</u>,
said the vet.

Draw a copy of spelling prompts from memory. Then cover your work before writing down the target word(s). Play Dicey Spellings to secure the new prompt pathways.

The cat with purple
fur is purring.

Spelling Tricks for Children by Sally Raymond

31

Draw a copy of the spelling prompt from memory. Then cover your work before writing down the target word(s). Play Dicey Spellings to secure the new prompt pathways.

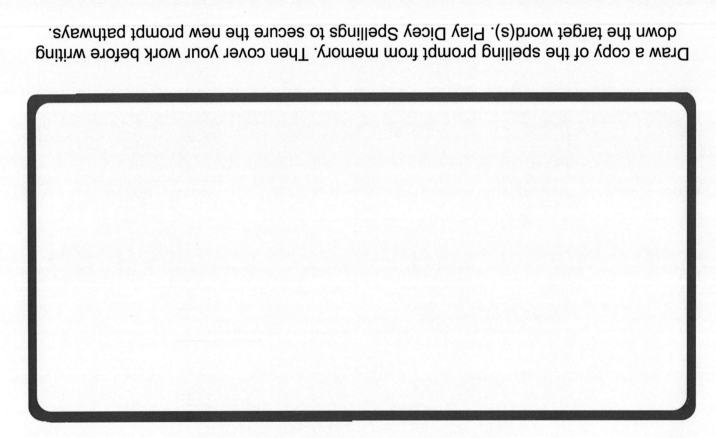

I saw a <u>mo</u>nster on <u>Mo</u>nday.

<u>U</u> <u>ea</u>t <u>s</u>weets on T<u>ue</u>sday.

I <u>wed</u> <u>Nes</u> on <u>Wed</u>nesday.

<u>U</u> <u>r</u>ide <u>s</u>heep on Th<u>urs</u>day.

<u>I</u> have sticky fingers on Friday.

<u>U</u> <u>r</u>ule the day on Sat<u>u</u>rday.

I have f<u>un</u> on S<u>un</u>day.

Monday

Tuesday

Wednesday

Thursday

Friday

SatUrday

Sunday

Spelling Tricks for Children by Sally Raymond   33

Draw a copy of spelling prompts from memory. Then cover your work before writing down the target word(s). Play Dicey Spellings to secure the new prompt pathways.

Spelling Tricks for Children by Sally Raymond

A green hairy tongue

is a horrible sight.

It gave me a fright when I turned on the light and saw that the knight had a green hairy tongue!

The knight didn't know how to knit. He was soon tied up in knots.

Draw a copy of spelling prompts from memory. Then cover your work before writing down the target word(s). Play Dicey Spellings to secure the new prompt pathways.

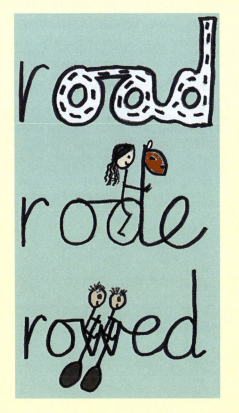

which hat

has fallen off

the witch?

Spelling Tricks for Children by Sally Raymond

37

Draw a copy of spelling prompts from memory. Then cover your work before writing down the target word(s). Play Dicey Spellings to secure the new prompt pathways.

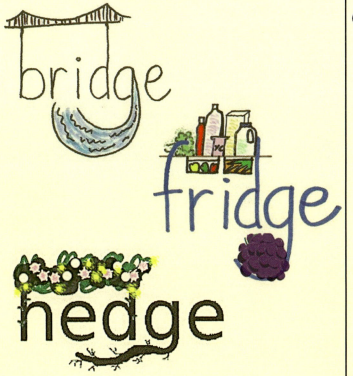

bridge

fridge

hedge

Our neighbour is British.

The Americans spell the word 'neighbor'.

neigh!

We know Nimble Eddie is growing hooves because our neighbour is a giant horse!

Draw a copy of spelling prompts from memory. Then cover your work before writing down the target word(s). Play Dicey Spellings to secure the new prompt pathways.

I will be your
friend to the end

Tomorrow is Monday.
We will be riding rhinos
borrowed in return for
a barrowful of marrows.

Draw a copy of spelling prompts from memory. Then cover your work before writing down the target word(s). Play Dicey Spellings to secure the new prompt pathways.

colour

flavour

odour

I ate both chocolate buttons.

Draw a copy of spelling prompts from memory. Then cover your work before writing down the target word(s). Play Dicey Spellings to secure the new prompt pathways.

wait   weight

As I **wait** at the bus stop my shopping bags feel like the **weight** of eight elephants!

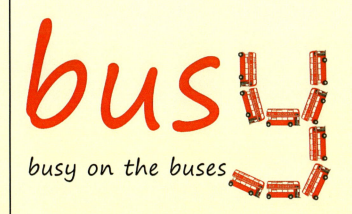

busy

busy on the buses

Spelling Tricks for Children by Sally Raymond

45

Draw a copy of spelling prompts from memory. Then cover your work before writing down the target word(s). Play Dicey Spellings to secure the new prompt pathways.

world

words

and round and round and round

worm

Shout OUT aloud

Library

You are all allowed
to talk in low voices

Draw a copy of spelling prompts from memory. Then cover your work before writing down the target word(s). Play Dicey Spellings to secure the new prompt pathways.

LÔÔK Ed!
He *looked*
your way!

Oh U greedy horse,
you have eaten right
through the gate!

Draw a copy of spelling prompts from memory. Then cover your work before writing down the target word(s). Play Dicey Spellings to secure the new prompt pathways.

head
l
m
p

Spot is a wonderful dog.

He likes to wander around the garden. I wonder what he is thinking about.

Draw a copy of spelling prompts from memory. Then cover your work before writing down the target word(s). Play Dicey Spellings to secure the new prompt pathways.

lau**gh**

and U giggle helplessly.

before (not befor)

Before ending,
add an e.

Draw a copy of spelling prompts from memory. Then cover your work before writing down the target word(s). Play Dicey Spellings to secure the new prompt pathways.

you — **O**pen **u**p **you**r **m**outh: ♪ sing! then ♪

final finally

real, really ta

Draw a copy of spelling prompts from memory. Then cover your work before writing down the target word(s). Play Dicey Spellings to secure the new prompt pathways.

wa ch

out

we went...

we were...

Write your own sentences.
Draw a picture for each one.

Draw a copy of spelling prompts from memory. Then cover your work before writing down the target word(s). Play Dicey Spellings to secure the new prompt pathways.

The **pea** made **peace** with the carrot by giving him a **piece** of caterpillar **pie**.

To small,

too **big**

and t**oo**

pink too.

Draw a copy of spelling prompts from memory. Then cover your work before writing down the target word(s). Play Dicey Spellings to secure the new prompt pathways.

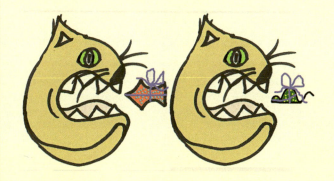

The car crash

was an accident

Two cats accept

their presents.

Draw a copy of spelling prompts from memory. Then cover your work before writing down the target word(s). Play Dicey Spellings to secure the new prompt pathways.

caravan   caravan   mushroom   mushroom

a<u>cc</u>o<u>mm</u>odation

Draw a copy of spelling prompts from memory. Then cover your work before writing down the target word(s). Play Dicey Spellings to secure the new prompt pathways.

I am

curious...

What makes you

furious?

monstr<u>ou</u>s <u>o</u>ctopuses
<u>u</u>psetting <u>sh</u>ips

... enorm<u>ous</u>, adventur<u>ou</u>s,
danger<u>ou</u>s <u>o</u>ctopuses
<u>u</u>psetting <u>sh</u>ips.

Spelling Tricks for Children by Sally Raymond

65

Draw a copy of spelling prompts from memory. Then cover your work before writing down the target word(s). Play Dicey Spellings to secure the new prompt pathways.

Spelling Tricks for Children by Sally Raymond

sCissOrs

palm

Spelling Tricks for Children by Sally Raymond

67

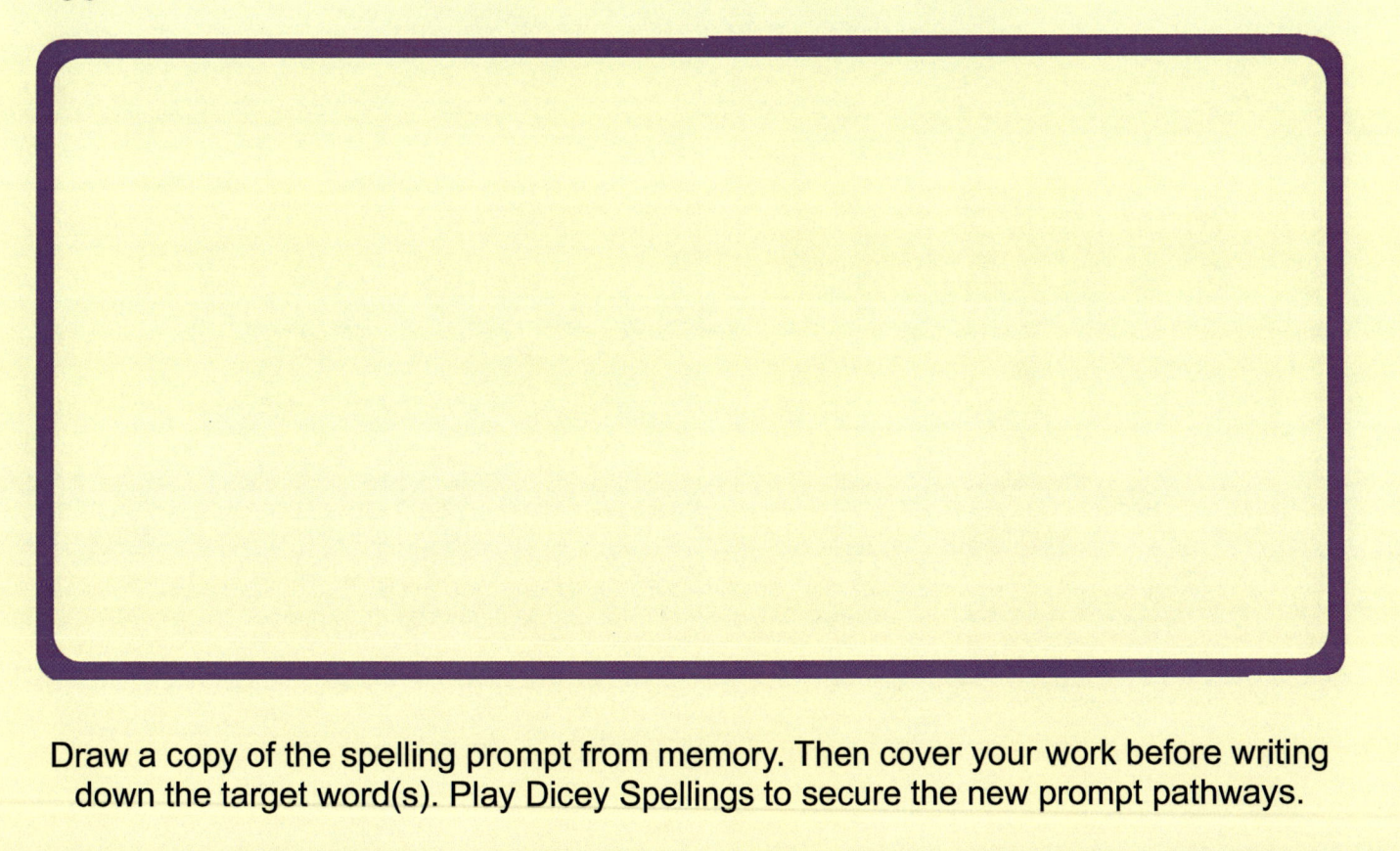

Draw a copy of the spelling prompt from memory. Then cover your work before writing down the target word(s). Play Dicey Spellings to secure the new prompt pathways.

A special _car_ is a lamborghini.

A special cat is a lynx.

A special cake is a lamington.

A lamington is a small square sponge cake coated with chocolate icing then dipped in desiccated coconut. A special treat!

Use the prompt you like best.

Draw a copy of spelling prompts from memory. Then cover your work before writing down the target word(s). Play Dicey Spellings to secure the new prompt pathways.

Spelling Tricks for Children by Sally Raymond

My daughter caught
An Ugly Green Hairy Trout

thumbs
up

HOORAY!

Spelling Tricks for Children by Sally Raymond

71

Draw a copy of spelling prompts from memory. Then cover your work before writing down the target word(s). Play Dicey Spellings to secure the new prompt pathways.

Bear is
w**ea**ring
emerald
and
ruby
earrings!

It can be difficult being
different said the flying
fish to the feathery flower.

Spelling Tricks for Children by Sally Raymond

73

Draw a copy of spelling prompts from memory. Then cover your work before writing down the target word(s). Play Dicey Spellings to secure the new prompt pathways.

guard

guess

guide

Ha**v**e you remembered
to add the *e*?

Spelling Tricks for Children by Sally Raymond

Draw a copy of spelling prompts from memory. Then cover your work before writing down the target word(s). Play Dicey Spellings to secure the new prompt pathways.

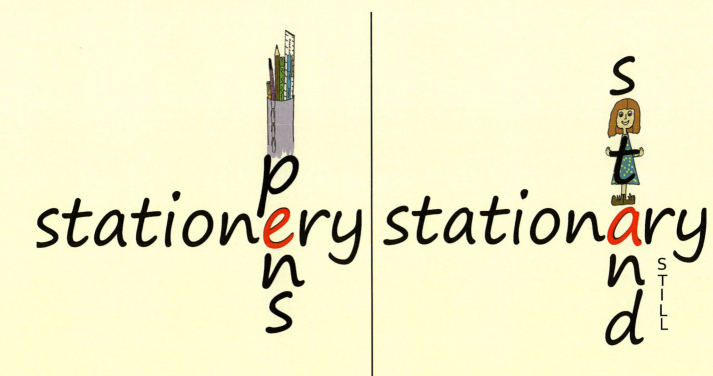

station**e**ry

station**a**ry

p
e
n
s

s
t
a
n
d STILL

Draw a copy of spelling prompts from memory. Then cover your work before writing down the target word(s). Play Dicey Spellings to secure the new prompt pathways.

EUrope

spells Europe

A siamese cat's roots are in Asia

Draw a copy of spelling prompts from memory. Then cover your work before writing down the target word(s). Play Dicey Spellings to secure the new prompt pathways.

many
ants
nick
yoghurt

few emus whistle

Spelling Tricks for Children by Sally Raymond

81

Draw a copy of spelling prompts from memory. Then cover your work before writing down the target word(s). Play Dicey Spellings to secure the new prompt pathways.

Come home
for some tea.

He chose
not to
lose a
rose up
his nose

Spelling Tricks for Children by Sally Raymond

83

Draw a copy of spelling prompts from memory. Then cover your work before writing down the target word(s). Play Dicey Spellings to secure the new prompt pathways.

Spelling Tricks for Children by Sally Raymond

84

This island
is land.

Oh U shouldn't touch
the grouch... ouch!

Draw a copy of spelling prompts from memory. Then cover your work before writing down the target word(s). Play Dicey Spellings to secure the new prompt pathways.

My mother's a moth.

No bother said my brother,

she looks like a Goth.

A STRAIT is a stretch of water joining two larger bodies of water. Add a giant hippo and get STRAIGHT into the news.

Giant Hippo Found in Strait.

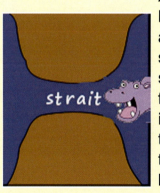

strait

A group of terrified locals reported seeing a giant hippo swimming towards the strait. Luckily, it was found to be an inflatable toy. Quickly, the coastguard towed the creature straight back to shore before it scared any tourists.

Draw a copy of spelling prompts from memory. Then cover your work before writing down the target word(s). Play Dicey Spellings to secure the new prompt pathways.

they're

They're playing volleyball.
Wow! **They are** winning!

draw - ward

<u>Draw</u> back<u>wards</u> to
spell for<u>wards</u>.

Draw a copy of spelling prompts from memory. Then cover your work before writing down the target word(s). Play Dicey Spellings to secure the new prompt pathways.

Spelling Tricks for Children by Sally Raymond

The **pirate** <u>ate</u>
rat pie.

Surely, lovely e is safely and securely placed... so why has 'truly' lost its e?

sorry

Draw a copy of the spelling prompt from memory. Then cover your work before writing down the target word(s). Play Dicey Spellings to secure the new prompt pathways.

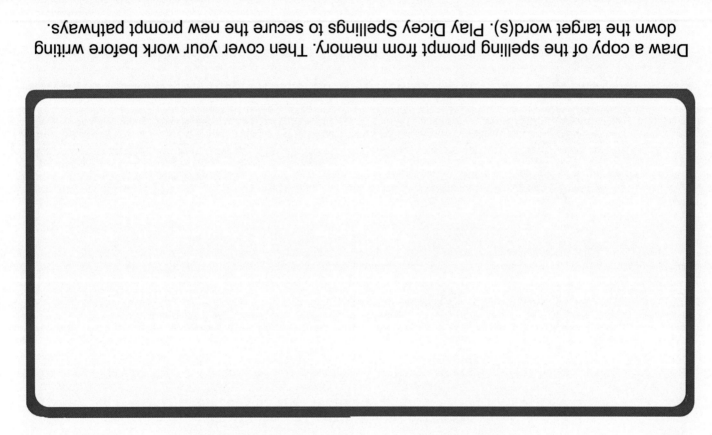

pic

Draw a picture of creature you might meet on an adventure.

Draw a copy of spelling prompts from memory. Then cover your work before writing down the target word(s). Play Dicey Spellings to secure the new prompt pathways.

<u>W</u>rap up <u>wr</u> to stop them <u>w</u>riggling.

<u>S</u>easons bring different weather whether <u>h</u>e likes it or not.

Spelling Tricks for Children by Sally Raymond

95

Draw a copy of spelling prompts from memory. Then cover your work before writing down the target word(s). Play Dicey Spellings to secure the new prompt pathways.

Spelling Tricks for Children by Sally Raymond

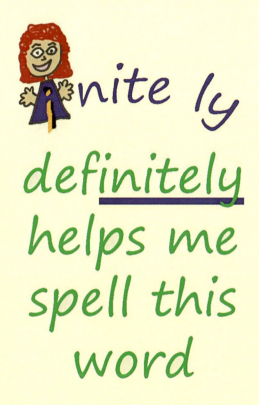

__fi__nite *ly*

definitely

helps me

spell this

word

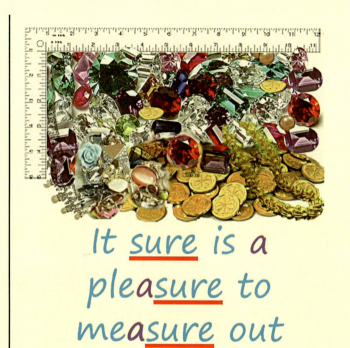

It <u>sure</u> is a ple<u>asure</u> to me<u>asure</u> out tre<u>asure</u>!

Spelling Tricks for Children by Sally Raymond

97

Draw a copy of spelling prompts from memory. Then cover your work before writing down the target word(s). Play Dicey Spellings to secure the new prompt pathways.

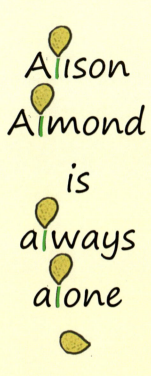

A**ll**son
A**l**mond
is
a**l**ways
a**l**one

asingle day in the life of an **a**phid.

Awake, **a**way, **a**bout, **a**long, **a**gain, **a**round, **a**ttack, **a**live, **a**mazing, **a**lways, **a**ltogether, **a**lready, **a**lso, **a**lmost, **a**sleep.

However, 'all right' is two words.

Draw a copy of spelling prompts from memory. Then cover your work before writing down the target word(s). Play Dicey Spellings to secure the new prompt pathways.

appear *disappear*

similar DisSImilaR

agree   disagree

Dear Miss Take,
We have made a **mistake**.
The words '...art and riches throughout your family history' should have read:
'Arton Riches threw out your family history'.
We are sorry for any **mis**understanding caused by the **mis**spelling of your family's **mis**fortune.
Yours sincerely,
Chris P. Bacon
Heir Born and Sons

Spelling Tricks for Children by Sally Raymond

101

Draw a copy of the spelling prompt from memory. Then cover your work before writing down the target word(s). Play Dicey Spellings to secure the new prompt pathways.

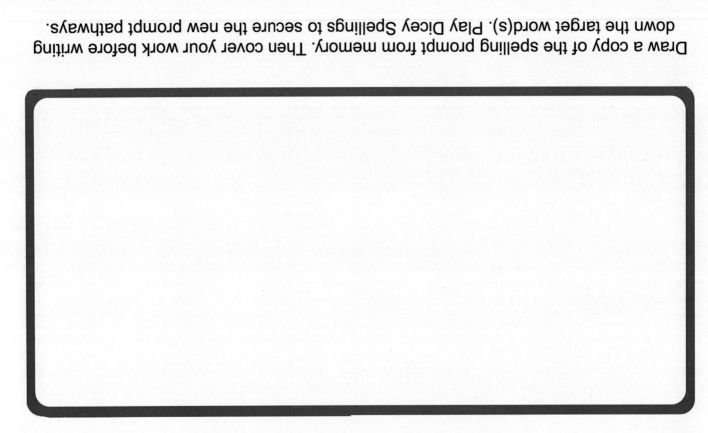

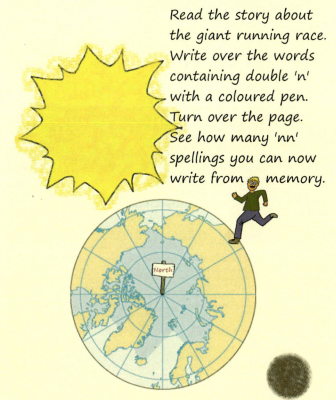

Read the story about the giant running race. Write over the words containing double 'n' with a coloured pen. Turn over the page. See how many 'nn' spellings you can now write from memory.

In the begiNNing, there was No Night-time.
It was always sunny, sunny, sunny.
Then Danny had an idea. He and Penny planned a giant running race to get the Earth spinning.
Granny pinned up a banner.
Nanny said she'd help them too, after dinner.
A cannon was fired to start them off. Jenny grinned as she took the lead, but then she fell into the Channel. She was annoyed, but Danny thought her seaweed hair was very funny.
"You're spinning!" announced the moon from above.
"A cunning plan and a stunning feat!"

In the begiNNing, there was No Night-time. But in the eND, Night and Day were connected side by side in an orderly manner.

Spelling Tricks for Children by Sally Raymond   103

When you meet new spellings which threaten to trip you up, use ideas from this book to help you invent your own prompts and accompanying pictures.

 Visit Dragonfly Teaching's Facebook page for more spelling tricks and materials.

Many thanks to my family and friends for all their encouragement and support during the writing of this book.

INDEX

Spelling Tricks for Children by Sally Raymond

moth	87	safely	91
mother	87	said	29
mouth	55	Saturday	33
		scissors	67
nanny	103	seasons	95
neighbour	39	securely	91
noise	23	see	9
nose	83	shouldn't	85
		shout	47
odour	43	sight	35
often	29	some	83
ouch	85	special	69
out	47	spinning	103
		stationary	77
palm	67	stationery	77
peace	59	straight	87
Penny	103	stunning	103
people	17	Sunday	33
picture	93	sunny	103
piece	59	sure	21
pinned	103	surely	91
pirate	91		
planned	103	talk	9
pleasure	97	tall	55
purple	31	their	19
purring	31	there	19
		they	27
really	55	they're	89
road	37	through	49
rode	37	thumb	71
rose	83	Thursday	33
rowed	37	tomorrow	41
running	103	too	59

touch	85	were	57
treasure	97	what	25
truly	91	when	27
Tuesday	33	whether	95
two	11	which	37
		who	25
wait	45	witch	37
walk	9	wonder	51
wander	51	wonderful	51
want	13	words	47
was	13	world	47
watch	57	worm	47
wearing	73	wrap	95
weather	95	wriggling	95
Wednesday	33		
weight	45	you	55
went	57	your	55

Many spelling mistakes can be blamed on the maddening nature of English spellings where identical letter patterns match 'said' with 'paid', 'know' with 'cow' and 'laugh' with 'caught'. Having learnt 'sort', it is then confusing to find 'bought', 'court' and 'taught' do not share similar letters. 'Head' and 'bead' look the same, but sound different; 'harm' and 'palm' look different but sound the same. It is a wonder that anyone can spell correctly, and it cannot be surprising to find 'pikcher', 'grate' instead of 'great', 'menny' and 'wot' appearing on the page.

If you are writing in Spanish, things are very different. As it is a transparent language, each sound (usually) uses the same letters across different words. This means spellings lack the 'plate', 'great', 'wait' and 'straight' variations which English contends with. If English was transparent (instead of opaque) then we might be spelling those words as 'plate', 'grate', 'wate' and 'strate'.

About 20% of the population find spellings harder to learn, remember and recall than their peers. This is nothing to do with intelligence (Einstein, amongst many great scientists and thinkers, was a poor speller), but due to the natural variation between different brains, and the complex nature of spelling development. If spelling ability was swapped with musical prowess we would probably find a similar variation of ability, with a different set of people struggling to succeed when asked to sing their CV(!)

Spelling Tricks for Children is designed to support spelling achievement by enhancing the processes required to create accurate and accessible spelling memories, especially for words containing misleading elements. Not all learners will find the same words difficult, or make the same mistakes. Adapt, whenever necessary, to suit individual needs.

Colourful, engaging and meaningful prompts help signpost spellers around the tripping hazards which lurk within many English spellings. The primary objective is for spellers to **LEARN and REMEMBER the SPELLING PROMPTS** for specific words. These, in turn, lead them to recall an accurate spelling trace. Over time, some prompts may not be needed, but for many, these spelling signposts remain as secure, reliable and long-lasting guides.

For tricky spellings to be recalled during written compositions, **the prompt pathway MUST be attached to the meaning of the word.** Additional elements such as grammar and etymology (word derivations) are hugely useful, but it is the meaning of a word, along with its sound (which can be misleading) which is triggered when words are being transcribed.

Spelling Tricks for Children enhances salient elements of a spelling by adding colour (which fires more neurons); identifying purpose (by spotlighting pitfalls); drawing from memory (recalling and repeating key elements of a prompt); ownership (learner produces own copy of prompts reproduced in their own hand); and repetition (playing Dicey Spellings reuses memory pathways to help establish them in the mind).

Other aspects of the spelling tricks include:

- The use of emotion: 'Sally-Anne is dead, said the vet', is far more effective than 'Sally-Ann is dancing.' Emotions such as disgust, horror, surprise, and delight add depth and strength to a memory trace. And having the word 'said' in the prompt ensures the learner knows which word the trick is helping them to spell.

- A novelty event requiring a thought-provoking depth of processing (e.g.'are aardvarks really extraterrestrials?') helps to overrule spelling errors which have become hard-to-shift habits.

- Interest certainly scores highly. 'A special car is a Lamborghini' may immediately secure the spelling of 'special' for some, but won't work as well for someone with no interest in cars.

- Clarity of purpose is also very important. 'Learn your spellings' is a very vague instruction for those who find rote learning slips through their minds like sand. Exploring the messages within different prompts, adapting them where necessary, also enhances personal relevance.

Identify the different styles of memory prompt used in this book to help design future tricks. Help learners to discover their own learning preferences, and support their use of personalised processing strategies. Finally, revisit material on a regular basis to ensure new memory pathways are converted into secure memory highways to boost confidence and success.

Good luck to you all,

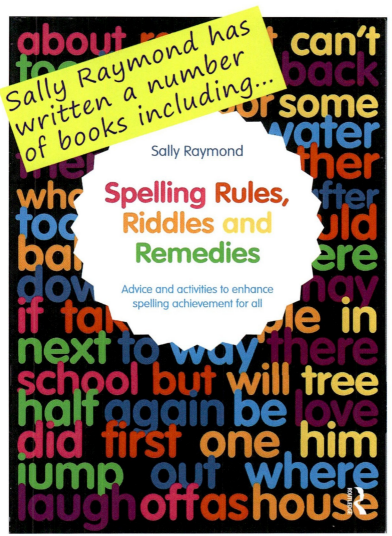

Sally Raymond has written a number of books including...

Sally Raymond

Spelling Rules, Riddles and Remedies

Advice and activities to enhance spelling achievement for all

ROUTLEDGE

Spelling Rules, Riddles and Remedies
- advice and activities to enhance spelling achievement

Published by Routledge (2015)

Spelling Tricks for Children

by Sally Raymond

is a book for those who want to:

- Get top marks in spelling.
- Avoid tripping over misleading sound-to-letter patterns which lurk within English spellings.
- Grin as you dodge common spelling mistakes.
- Explore and enjoy colourful and playful learning strategies.
- Master tricky spellings at a gentle and rewarding pace.

"My 8 yr old LOVES this book - she now *wants* to spell!"

"Fun, colourful, easy to follow. My son enjoys using these prompts. He likes discovering why he was making mistakes."

Published by Dragonfly Teaching

9 780995 476905